C000181810

Alternative Worship
in the
Church of England

Paul Roberts
Tutor in Worship and Doctrine, Trinity College, Bristol
Member of the *Third Sunday Service*, Bristol

GROVE BOOKS LIMITED
RIDLEY HALL RD CAMBRIDGE CB3 9HU

Contents

The Cover Illustration is by Peter Ashton

First Impression October 1999
ISSN 0144-1728
ISBN 1 85174 415 0

1

Introduction

Alternative worship has been around in the Church of England for over a decade. During this time, it has attracted interest, enthusiasm, suspicion and notoriety. Despite the exposure of the *Nine O'Clock Service* (*NOS*) as an abusive and cult-like group, significant numbers of people have continued to work with alternative worship across the country. The number of groups of these people has continued to grow since 1995. Some of them operate under the umbrella of Anglican parish churches. Increasingly, church leaders have started to look to alternative worship as a new way to reverse the decline in the church's ability to attract young adults and hold on to those who grew up through its youth work.

Generally speaking, however, alternative worship is not a form of youth work. Most of those involved are in their 20s and 30s. The ethos of most groups reflects a desire to grow in a mature adult expression of Christianity, rather than the need to cope with an adolescent transition from the faith of childhood.[1] Furthermore, alternative worship involves more than contemporary music, nightclub lighting and multi-media. Although it often uses these things, it has a wider agenda that embraces theology, the nature of church life, and how the gospel is applied in Christian proclamation and personal life.[2] It arises from the need for the church to engage with a culture shift, from the patterns of Christian life which took shape in modernity, to a faith which brings the authentic message of Christ to bear on life in postmodernity. This is a bold aim, which lends itself to creativity, experimentation and theological reflection. On the other hand, it can sometimes lead to groups becoming over-intellectual, angry, introspective, volatile, and lacking in a strategic approach to mission—all classical problems of would-be revolutionary groups. Yet alternative worship attracts many who would have stood out as obvious Christian leaders in more usual church contexts. They have refused to follow the route into Christian leadership because they perceive a growing gulf between the agenda presently pursued by the wider church and the spiritual needs expressed within the culture of their peers. These needs, which they also find reflected in themselves, are not being met by the worship, spirituality, politics and mission agenda of mainstream church life.

Although not youth-oriented, alternative worship is a 'young' movement since it reflects the cultural changes that are pressing hardest on younger people. The 1980s were not a good decade for young people in the Church of England. Ten years on, it has become apparent that church decline is most severe among teenagers and the young adult population of the country. The voice of the young is

---

1   See Patrick Angier, *Changing Youth Worship* (London: National Society/CHP, 1997).
2   A number of churches have started to do 'Youth,' or 'Generation-X' services in this way, but they have not fostered innovation beyond the external trappings of worship.

largely drowned within the church by older voices. This has political consequences that affect a range of aspects of national and local church life, including mission and worship. It is therefore important for the church to listen to those creative groups who are most engaged with the culture of the younger end of the adult populace. Alternative worship has an enormous contribution to make to the church's mission as our society is progressively affected by the cultural changes that are currently most acutely affecting the younger half of the population. The need to hear and the need to speak are pressing.

The term 'alternative worship' is unfortunate. Many groups reject the term in favour of something more descriptive.[3] However, like the name 'charismatic,' which can be equally confusing, it has become the term that is most widely recognized to refer to the phenomenon under discussion. Therefore, this book will continue to use the term 'alternative worship' without further comment.

---

3   'Creative worship.' 'New worship' and 'Postmodern worship' have all been used.

2

What is Alternative Worship Like?

The best way of discovering more about alternative worship is to go along to a service. However, the title 'alternative worship' has been used to cover a wide variety of types of worship. For example, an internet web search engine will yield a host of different kinds of sites describing 'alternative' worship. Yet many of these—especially those in America—are merely describing something that uses contemporary music, drama and discussion while following the same set of liturgical assumptions as a standard service. So in the interests of clarification, we shall look at some common characteristics of that family of worship services which are often described in Britain, New Zealand and Australia as 'alternative worship.'

A Multi-media Environment Resulting from Intense Creativity
If someone who is used to other forms of worship walks into an alternative worship service, they often spend the first few minutes not knowing where to look or what to focus on. Projected images, physical objects, words, music, smells and movement may all be happening simultaneously. Sometimes the plethora of points of focus is deliberately designed to obscure a single point of focus—so that people are given the freedom to locate their attention on a point of choice. At other times, they are designed to co-ordinate, so that a single point is elaborated using different media.

When each of the media is considered singly, they are normally the fruit of considerable amounts of local creativity. As much creative energy is put into framing the words of prayers as goes into putting together other aspects of the service. Creativity is also the name of the game elsewhere—in home-produced or home-edited video, Super-8 projections, slides, paintings, music, and so on.

The Use of Visuals
The use of the visual media occurs through paintings, drawings, sculpture, projected slides, cine and video footage. Here are some examples from actual services:
- Two huge, colourful, slightly abstract banners, hanging from the roof, painted on fabric.
- The construction during the service of a fifteen-foot-high crucifix from junk taken from a skip (using hammers, nails, and electric drill).
- Slides of cityscapes projected on screens which enclosed the worship space entirely, giving a slightly agoraphobic sensation with their sudden arrival.
- A black and white Super-8 cine loop of cartoons of candles, dancing around the screen.
- An edited and 'looped' sequence of a swinging incense thurible.

The symbolism contained in the visuals varies in its degree of abstraction. One example of direct symbolism is the use of broken chains and liberated animals to speak of absolution/forgiveness, but more abstract symbolism is also used. Traditional Christian icons, from both East and West, are also popular subject material. Sometimes words (usually single words) are projected.

The sources for these visuals are various. In many cases they are home-produced by those who are running the service, but use is also made of readily available sources such as music videos, clips from television, dance videos, and photographs from books.

Art installations also feature in some of the more developed services, and sometimes provide the entire context of the worship service itself. The best known example is the *labyrinth*, modelled on Christian labyrinths such as that found in Chartres Cathedral. In an alternative worship labyrinth, a single pathway snakes around a complex symmetrical pattern, usually laid out on the floor. At locations in the labyrinth, written guidance or drawings are placed to help individuals pray as they pass through it. The labyrinth thus forms a metaphor for life: at points in it we encounter God in different ways, finding him accompanying us on our journey. The installation aspect of the labyrinth has been expanded in Bristol's *Third Sunday Service* by being surrounded by a rectangular box of sheeting from the floor upwards. Upon these sheets are projected various moving and static images (including words). Music plays throughout the service. Sometimes words are read over the PA. Since not everyone can get in the labyrinth simultaneously, other visual points of focus ('stations') which use art, sculpture, reading and the option to light candles, wash, or write may be provided. There is also a café/bar at one end of the worship space for quiet conversations whilst the labyrinth is in operation.

Because of the extensive use made of projections and sources of light (candles and fire) it is common for such services to take place in the dark. This may also be influenced by the background culture of the club, and also the fact that the services normally happen in later evening, which is a convenient time for most young adults. Nevertheless, over more recent years a number of services have taken to using daylight contexts as well—and even worshipping out of doors.

Use of Sound

Sometimes the music of alternative worship is there to be listened to; sometimes it is merely there for background effect. The latter use explains the use of 'ambient' music. The notion of ambient music comes from the work of the experimental pop musician Brian Eno, whose series of albums beginning with *Music for Airports* began a genre that uses electronic instruments and sampling to produce abstract but rather pleasing music. It lends itself particularly well to the spiritually-attuned environment of worship.

Some (though not all) alternative worship congregations have dancing. In these groups, either recordings of secular dance music are pressed into service or sometimes music is written and performed specially. There is a tendency (not a new one) to reinterpret the lyrics of secular songs in the worship context. Some secular dance songs have explicitly spiritual, even Christian lyrics. Other club artists are Christians producing dance music that sometimes has a spiritual focus.[4]

Unlike the charismatic renewal, alternative worship has not produced a burst of new choruses or hymns. Generally it is much more restrained in its use of singing. One reason for this is that some people associate singing lots of choruses with their charismatic background or childhood, so react negatively to this element within worship. This reaction against choruses also explains the preference for meditative chants rather than 'exuberant' or 'slushy' choruses. Some services have produced tapes and CDs, but only some of the material is suitable for congregational singing.[5] One other method has been to write new tunes to old hymns.[6]

How Are Services Led?

One of the most distinguishing marks of alternative worship is that it refuses to assign a single presidential role, but uses technology to allow a service to be 'steered' using vocal instruction, prayers, slide/video announcements and the use of multiple voices. There is a strong resistance to the cult of personality that has tended to grow up in the charismatic renewal around the worship leader. It would be both unthinkable and impossible for alternative worship to produce a worship album with a name of a single artist on it. The entire method of leading and directing worship militates against this. Very often the person who is 'on microphone' is invisible to the congregation. Music is so often prerecorded that there is no 'audience/performer' interaction implicit in the course of worship. An exception can be communion services, where denominational tradition is often followed, although sometimes with two or more people co-presiding. Other groups celebrate communion as a simple meal, where different people pray prayers of thanksgiving. Generally, microphones are used as democratically as possible.

Despite this resistance towards presidency, explicit and implicit ritual roles continue to exist within alternative worship. For those congregations that have a connection to club culture, the DJ acts as both provider of music and also master of ceremonies (in both the liturgical and club senses of the term). Sometimes members of the planning group will initiate discussion groups, welcome and bid farewell to people, or may ceremonially bring in offerings (for example, the eucharistic elements, oil, fire).

---

4 The American producer/DJ Moby expresses a vehement, off-beat, anti-fundamentalist, pro-vegetarian version of Christianity.

5 One good example is Charlie Irvine's 'Author of Creation' on Music from the *Late Late Service 4—God in the Flesh* (Sticky Music, CD–GUMCD27, 1994).

6 *Grace's* CD, *Eucharist* contains a version of *St Patrick's Breastplate* by Richard Wheeler of TSS. LLS recorded *O come, O come Immanuel* (*Music from the Late Late Service 4—God in the Flesh*), and *Swing low sweet chariot* (*Music from the Late Late Service 3*, Sticky Music, CD–GUM25CD, 1993).

What is the Congregation Doing?

The following activities can commonly be found in alternative worship services:

- Making things
- Singing chants
- Body praying (using sequences of bodily positions in connection with either a theme or a simple prayer which is prayed silently)
- Discussion
- Writing
- Taking part in ritual actions—either corporately or individually
- Laying on one's back staring at the ceiling
- Dancing
- Silent prayer
- Gazing at images or candles
- Watching TV
- Eating and drinking

Sometimes these things are prescribed by an announcement, but quite often there is a good deal of leeway in what people are expected to be doing. Verbal directions tend to sound more like suggestions than instructions. Again, this style has often developed in deliberate contrast to the prescriptive style of leading worship in churches having a strong group pressure towards ritual conformity.

Liturgical Sources and Resources

Although the final product of an alternative worship service is the result of considerable activity on the ground, other resources from outside the community and within it are used. The *Late Late Service* was the first to produce tapes specifically designed to stimulate other groups into creativity or to resource them.[7] Services have used Taizé, Iona and Gelineau chants, even traditional Gregorian chant in Latin set to plainsong tones. *Grace* (London) became the first to sell videotapes designed for use in worship services. Besides selling CD and video resources, most alternative worship communities are quite free in sharing what other resources they have produced—especially music and prayers. In 1997 the 'Alternative Worship FAQ' web-site was set up to facilitate this.[8]

The words and liturgies of alternative worship are normally home-grown. However, since a lot of services are influenced by modern Celtic spirituality, traditional Celtic or Celtic-inspired rites are sometimes used. The ready-made liturgies of mainstream churches tend only to be used when circumstances insist. The main reason for this seems to be that the language is too non-specific, too empty

---

7   The sleeve notes of *Music from the Late Late Service 2* (Sticky Music, Tape–GUM20MC, 1992) explicitly state both resourcing and stimulating creativity as their aim.
8   http://www.trinity-bris.ac.uk/altw_faq.

of emotion or too wordy, and the rites assume things that do not work in multi-media contexts.

Since creativity is part of the essence of alternative worship, there is a tension between producing in order to stimulate others whilst discouraging the passive use of ready-made resources. This is why the resources of alternative worship services have not developed into a market, nor are they likely to for the foreseeable future.

Does It All Hang Together?

Given the complicated nature of an act of alternative worship, it is only fair to look at the pitfalls into which these services can easily fall. There are two classic problems:

- Services can be over-didactic, where a theme is not explored using sufficient media resources, where the congregation is treated like a passive audience, and inadequate opportunity or instruction is given for participation.
- Services can be chaotic, where the congregation have little option other than to watch, and try to make sense of it all.

In both these cases, the resulting problem is the same. The congregation is not engaged properly, leading to the event failing to function fully as an act of worship.

On the other hand, when services work properly, the following qualities can be observed:

- A healthy avoidance of personality cult, and the development of harmonious ritual performance across the group.
- The creative and effective use of technology to ensure minimum interruption to the flow of worship.
- Careful thinking about which medium is most effective to use in moving people through the event as a single congregation.
- As sense of unhurried space, where people sense the presence of God in the midst of imaginative beauty.
- A sense of belonging and engagement by all present without being at the expense of personal integrity.

Groups doing alternative worship are faced with a demanding environment in which to operate ritual effectively. Those who lead services in more 'traditional' church contexts will know well how difficult it is to marshal all the different components of a service together into a harmonious whole. This challenge is much greater in the complex multi-media environment of alternative worship. Yet *when* it works, it is an astonishing and inspiring thing to behold and in which to participate.

3
History

Alternative worship in Britain traces its origins to the formation of the *Nine O'Clock Service* in Sheffield in the late 1980s.[9] *NOS* began as a worship service following John Wimber's visit to Sheffield in 1985. Its unique style of worship, which aimed at expressing radical, evangelical Christianity in the cultural forms of a nightclub had an immediate impact on the young adult Christians of Sheffield. The service trebled in numbers during its first year. By the end of the 1980s, *NOS* was attracting hundreds of people, many of whom were young adults who had grown up in churches affected by evangelicalism and charismatic renewal. For this generation of young adult Christians, the culture of their home churches, expressed in worship and social mores, was embarrassing and jaded. They discovered in *NOS* an apparently perfect combination of radical Christian discipleship and worship expressed in the new multi-media format that was becoming state of the art club culture. As a result, many moved to Sheffield to join the community, while still more regularly travelled hundreds of miles for a 'fix' of worship which inspired them in their faith and gave them a rare sense of being 'at home' in church.

It was among this group of *NOS* 'commuters' that the seeds of other services were born. *NOS* provided the lead, but others quickly followed. Yet *NOS* was, from its inception, very suspicious of imitators and shunned links with other alternative worship communities, who consequently had to learn to stand on their own feet.[10] By the early 1990s, a number of other services had started. The most significant of these was the *Late Late Service* who held very influential services at the Greenbelt arts festival from 1992 onwards and were first to publish their own worship tapes which provided a source and inspiration for others trying to do the same thing. *LLS* was founded by a group of Glasgow-based musicians following a successful attempt at doing 'alternative worship' at a diocesan youth event in Edinburgh. They were given space to do this by St Silas', an Episcopalian church with an evangelical tradition in Glasgow. However, since *LLS*'s founding members came from a number of denominations, it was an ecumenical, self-governing project from its inception. Unlike *NOS*, who inherited an 'inspired and divinely-elected leader' theology from Wimber's charismatic Vineyard Churches, *LLS* was fiercely democratic in nature, reflecting both the polity of Scottish Presbyterianism and charismatic renewal's relative lack of influence north of the border.

Greenbelt formed a point of contact for individuals and groups starting up alternative worship projects. It was here in 1993 that alternative worship began to

---

9 For the story of *NOS*, see Roland Howard, *The Rise and Fall of the Nine O'Clock Service* (London: Mowbray, 1996). The residual members of *NOS* continue to meet as the Nine O'clock Community (NoC).

10 This explains why other alternative worship services in Britain did not collapse in the wake of the end of *NOS*.

take on an international dimension, with a visit by Mark Pierson, a Baptist pastor who had begun an alternative worship service at his church in New Zealand. Groups began to network together, and a couple of day conferences were held at the Greenhouse in London. As the internet was beginning to open up, far-flung groups were able to stay in touch through email discussion lists. Nevertheless, although isolated services had begun in New Zealand and Australia, Britain dominated the field. A number of services founded between 1990 and 1994 remain in existence, including *LLS*, *Visions*[11] (planted from St Michael-le-Belfry), *Third Sunday Service* (*TSS*) in Bristol, *The Mass*[12] (Long Eaton), and *Joy* (Oxford).

NOS, however, remained in the vanguard in terms of liturgical innovation and (to a lesser extent) theological influence. When they produced a new 'Planetary Mass' in 1993, a number of its features were imported into alternative worship services elsewhere. Their move away from charismatic theology towards the writings of Matthew Fox was reflected by a number of other services. Fox attended the British alternative worship conference in 1995 on hearing that *NOS* were not alone in doing creative ritual. However, following the collapse of *NOS*, his influence has tended to be less prominent.

Harry

If *NOS* marks a point of origin, a second strand in the history of alternative worship in Britain comes from the direction of the house churches and the *Harry* arts festival. This was initiated by Dave Tomlinson, who at one time had been an apostle in one of the Restoration groups and remained an influential, if controversial figure, in the house church scene throughout the early 1990s. *Harry* was an arts festival geared particularly to the rising generation of Christians who had grown up in the house churches. A significant number of this second-generation had struggled to remain within their parents' churches, for cultural and theological reasons. Among the house churches, fundamentalism, authoritarian leadership styles and pre-millennialism had exerted more influence than in mainstream denominational charismatic churches. *Harry* allowed these younger Christians free space to explore doubts and alternative theological solutions in ways that would not be tolerated in the more restricted environment of their home churches. As part of its cultural and theological space, *Harry* adopted a very experimental approach to worship, which—while remaining experiential—explored the use of symbol, story and discussion in a way unheard of in mainstream charismatic worship.[13] Over time, Tomlinson became a point of refuge for young adults whose faith and life experiences could no longer be comfortably situated within the conservative house church context. He began a series of off-beat meetings in a pub in South London which became known as *Holy Joe's*, studied for a masters' degree in theology, and was eventually received and ordained into the Church of England.

---

11 Formerly 'Warehouse.'
12 Formerly 'Be Real.'
13 See Dave Tomlinson, *The Post-evangelical* (London: SPCK, 1996).

The worship services of *Harry* and *Holy Joe's* both reflected the same kind of attention to symbol, ritual, music and multi-media which were happening in other alternative worship services. Some from *Harry* had attended *NOS*, but at the start of the 1990s there was still a strong enough sense of gulf between 'restoration' approaches to church (which in effect suggested that denominational churches are obsolete) and that of the mainstream to keep the two groups formally distinct. However, when Tomlinson published *The Post-evangelical* it became apparent that the agenda he was exploring resonated with many second-generation charismatics, irrespective of denomination. It also offered a more broad-church, yet orthodox theology than the Fox-oriented radicalism of *NOS*, which some within alternative worship were rather unhappy with.[14]

The Collapse of NOS

With the exposure and collapse of *NOS*, the immediate feeling within most alternative worship groups was a mixture of profound pity and shock. There was also a sense of having one's worst suspicions realized, since the isolationism of *NOS*, together with stories about its 'heavy' leadership, had been ringing alarm-bells for some time. By 1995 there were enough established groups to maintain a sense of equilibrium throughout the crisis. A matter of only weeks later, the Archbishop of Canterbury courageously allowed a study day on alternative worship for the House of Bishops and heads of church boards to go ahead. This had been planned some months previously by his adviser on youth, Pete Ward. The day started with an alternative worship communion service in the crypt of Lambeth Palace which had been put together by representatives of *Visions*, *TSS*, *Be Real*, *Abundant* (London) and *Joy*. Practitioners had written a number of accompanying descriptive and theological papers. The day helped in a number of ways: it showed that alternative worship was not to be equated exclusively with *NOS*; that the abuses within *NOS* were a function of its unique hierarchical leadership structure, rather than its liturgy; and that there was considerable diversity of theology and practice within the various groups. It made a strong case that alternative worship was a creative movement that should be encouraged, albeit with the caution born of painful experience.

The exposure of *NOS* was probably the most embarrassing event to happen to the Church of England during the 1990s, so it is not surprising that members of the hierarchy of the Church have not raced into public identification with groups that look similar. However, there has been a steady growth of the number of alternative worship in succeeding years. Many remain quite small, and some 'burn out' after a few years. But where there has been good leadership and a willingness to foster them by local churches, larger and long-lasting communities have come into existence. A number of congregations exist either within or under the auspices of Anglican churches, which continue to develop creative acts of wor-

---

14 Doug Gay, a founder of *LLS*, publicly disputed with Fox's theology during the latter's visit to the 1995 York Conference.

ship, witness to cultures far-removed from church life, and pastor people who struggle to belong to more mainstream congregations. *Elemental*, a constituent group of the Bristol consortium *Third Sunday Service*, have run a Christian spirituality tent at the Glastonbury pop festival for the past three years. Groups remain in touch globally by the email list, altw@tmtm.com, and meet regularly at events such as Greenbelt. After years of being the home of haphazard small or short-lived experiments, London now has a good number of groups who work together across denominational lines.[15] In 1999, as part of the Archbishop of Canterbury's celebration, *The Time of Our Lives*, an alternative worship service was held in South-wark Cathedral, and alternative worship groups took a creative role alongside leaders of other worship styles in the final eucharist.[16]

Alternative worship continues to thrive in Australia and New Zealand.[17] There are also signs that it is being discovered by a number of mainstream churches in the United States. In an important article in the online version of *Leadership* magazine, Daniel M Harrell, associate pastor at Park Street Church, Boston MA describes how the 1980s-style seeker-friendly services were no longer effective in attracting younger adults. 'Whatever the reason, many younger leaders are turning from seeker-sensitive forms toward recapturing *ambiguity* and *antiquity*.'[18] He continues to describe how the policy of his church changed in 1997:

> So we set aside our seeker strategy and intensified our eclectic style of Anglo-catholic liturgical cues, Pentecostal rock-n-roll rhythms, high-tech seques, Reformed preaching, and Quaker collectiveness.[19]

Although reflecting the different context of American Christianity, there are enough similarities in this description to see a resemblance to British and Australasian forms of alternative worship.

---

15 These include *Grace* (St Mary's, Ealing), *Epicentre* (St Mark's, Battersea Rise), *Holy Joe's*, *The Host Community* (URC, Powerscroft Chapel in Hackney) and *Vaux* (St Peter's, Kennington Road).
16 Music at the eucharist was provided by a choir led by Geoff Weaver of the RSCM, and by Matt Redman from *Soul Survivor*, while backing ambience was mixed by Jonny Baker (*Grace*) and the author (*Third Sunday Service*).
17 A number of groups are springing up in Australia, for example, *Café Church* and *Plunge* both meet in Sydney, *Late Late Service* in Adelaide. While in New Zealand, there is *Parallel Universe* (Auckland), *Soul Outpost* (Dunedin), *eXpresso* (Christchurch) among many others.
18 http://www.christianity.net/leadership/9L2/9L2037.html
19 *ibid.*

4
Philosophy

Since no two alternative worship services share a liturgical text, it is far more appropriate to describe a shared 'philosophy' of alternative worship. At its heart, *alternative worship is a creative event arising from a community of Christians*. It is this emphasis on *group creativity* that accounts for the main features of alternative worship. Because it happens as an *event*, in one sense nothing 'precedes' the worship at all—there is no written text, or standard set of roles. Indeed, for many of those who are regularly hard at work creating alternative worship, the offering of the *process* often eclipses the event itself as an act of worship.

The Text of Worship

There are parallels between alternative worship and postmodern theories of art and literature. Put as simply as possible, postmodernism does not regard a text (be it literary or artistic) as a fixed object. The 'text' has permeable boundaries that include the time and context of the reader or viewer, and the place and time in which it is displayed or read. Thus, in postmodern theory, the traditional distinction between reader and text becomes blurred. Likewise, in alternative worship, the 'text' of the worship is unbounded—embracing the activities and spontaneities of the participants as part of the whole. In postmodern art, this kind of thinking has led to a relentless drive to move beyond the picture frame, through the use of performance art and multi-media installations that occur in 'real time.' In alternative worship the act of worship is not mediated by any single medium, but takes place as a multi-media ritual. As such, no single element of the rite takes any precedence over another, be it words, music, singing, or visuals. This is reinforced by the fact that any number of these things can be happening simultaneously. One radical expression of this is when worship occurs through means of 'installations,' labyrinths or 'stations.' In these, the act of worship is operating in ways similar to a contemporary art installation, which needs its 'viewers' in order to function properly as a complete work of art.

The reason alternative worship has followed contemporary art has more to do with the changing relationship between art and popular culture, than because of an effete desire to produce 'arty' worship. In the mid-1980s, radical art collectives became involved with setting up warehouse parties.[20] This in turn opened up the dance culture to a new co-operation between DJs and radical artists, producing parties and raves having a strong element of performance art within them. Music had been going along this path for some years previously, as the role of the DJ had expanded to include scratching, sampling and rapping, rather than just putting

---

20 A classic example is the activity of various art collectives in the lead-up to the closure of the Greater London Council.

on records. Many of those currently involved with alternative worship have had close links with this movement in dance culture. So, in alternative worship, it is not uncommon to see a DJ having a key role in producing the ritual environment 'live' using decks and samplers. He or she is doing a similar thing to a good organist improvising during the communion at mass. The art of young contemporary culture blurs the distinction between art, performance and joyful celebration. So it is natural that this blurring should affect the celebration of Christian worship. However, within alternative worship a distinctively Christian appreciation of what is going on has also emerged.

The Bible in Alternative Worship

This process of liturgical creativity is the location for the group's encounter with the Bible. It is typically an exercise in shared interpretation, as the creative group seeks to develop an understanding of themselves and the world around them with the aid of the Bible. This is often forced on the group by the need to crystallize their interpretation into creative expressions of worship the following Sunday—in other words, a 'Bible study in desperation' familiar to most preachers! One typical effect of this process is that Bible study becomes very interactive, both within the group and within the services. A second effect is how quickly such groups become open to forms of radical but highly practical interpretation, which contrast starkly with the received orthodoxies in which many of their members were nurtured. For example, conservative approaches to the Bible may be questioned, as too may some inherited assumptions about structures of church authority, or the place of women. There may be a new emphasis on the social component of the gospel. Experience suggests that this is coming about through a group-focussed interpretation of the Bible in a contemporary setting, rather than through the imposition of an external, 'liberal' agenda. Before too long, Bible study in most groups becomes a place when there are no 'forbidden zones' where questions cannot be asked of the text.

What is most interesting from the liturgical viewpoint is how the creative group is taking on the homiletical role of the preacher, including the struggle to apply the biblical text to the ordinary life of the worshippers. A common, if demanding question to answer is 'what image or piece of music could capture the message of this text?' It is this approach, embracing affective and well as cognitive biblical study, which has made the Bible come alive again in the context of shared liturgical creativity.

Who Is It For?

To have any integrity, alternative worship services must be 'for' those who are engaged in creating them and worshipping within them. Many churches often miss this point, seeing alternative worship merely as an opportunity to attract young 'outsiders' into the church through using popular culture. It has often proved very hard for Christians who wish to start alternative worship services to be able to do so without selling the idea as little more than trendy evangelism.

Whatever the stated reason for starting up, these groups need to see what they are doing as their own spirituality, rather than as worship by proxy. This can lead the host church to feel less enthusiastic, because it rightly sees a potential challenge to their integration *back* into *normal* Sunday worship. Ultimately this is the problem of reconciling the need for fully inculturated worship with the fact that our Western societies contain huge sub-cultural diversity. So which goes out— inculturation or the need to have a supposedly multi-cultural symbolic expression in every act of Sunday morning worship?

'Heaven in Ordinarie'

By blurring the distinction between the act of worship and its production, alternative worship groups develop a spirituality that lays great store in offering creativity to God as the essence of worship. This is a strongly incarnational spirituality, which enacts through its worship the offering up of the mundane—the totality and ordinariness of our human lives. If this is so, then alternative worship has more in common with a more 'catholic' approach to worship than the charismatic emphasis on the 'ecstatic' experience in worship.[21]

This incarnational spirituality has an understanding of Christian community which emphasizes its openness to those others whose faith commitment may not yet be or may no longer be recognizably Christian. Many within alternative worship would state this as a primary reason for their involvement: to belong to a church community where Christian commitment is not set in any opposition to full engagement with the society beyond its bounds. They want services to which they can take friends without acute embarrassment, indeed, services with which they can be proud to be identified. There is something profoundly 'Anglican' in this instinct, even when it occurs among non-Anglican groups. An understanding of mission, which focuses on worship which both embraces people of faith, and also is appealing to people who may have no faith, has long had a home in Anglican consciousness. The Church of England, as a national church, traditionally sought to be a church that embraced the lax as well as the fervent. It sees the church not as the gathered company of confessors, but as an open institution with permeable boundaries. It embraces and welcomes, defining itself through its worship, rather than through credal subscription. This has a good deal in common with the ethos of alternative worship groups, many of whom welcome people of belief and of no belief to participate in their worship. In this way, they are reacting against an 'in your face' approach to church identity and evangelism associated with a church-versus-world understanding.

A Postmodern Worship Experience

Though less interested in (and perhaps cynical of) the ecstatic emphasis of charismatic worship, alternative worship still holds experience to be important.

---

21 For a classic 'catholic' exposition of this theology, see R Hebert, *Liturgy and Society* (London: Faber and Faber, 1935).

Coming into God's presence, and knowing—experientially—that you are there, is the aim of good worship. This suggests that alternative worship is a development from a charismatic base, but with considerable change brought about through the process of inculturation into the postmodern context.

On the other hand, it is common to find experiences of 'God's presence' within alternative worship to be radically demythologized. Alternative worshippers are likely to be quite open minded about whether to ascribe their experiences to God, or to psychological factors within the rite which made them feel 'as though' God were particularly present. Some of the services show clear evidence of having been put together by people who have been influenced by the phenomenological approaches of social anthropology in their understanding of how 'rites' function. Rituals within alternative worship are often quite deliberately designed for the impact they will have on the worshippers present, without any intention to manipulate by subterfuge. This is also why it is much more common to hear people within alternative worship describing their worship as 'a ritual' rather than as 'worship' in order to emphasize the conscious hand they have had in creating an experiential environment.

5

Where Is It All Coming From?

When a group of young Christians say that they want to start an alternative worship service, they are frequently met with blank faces on the part of other church members. There is a genuine difficulty in communicating what it is they are intending to do differently. Why do they wish to do this? Why are they not content with the worship currently on offer? This is particularly so if they belong to a charismatic or lively evangelical church, since such churches have got used to seeing themselves as in the vanguard of youthful, relevant worship. When the members of the group start to explain what they want to do, a good deal of it sounds uncomfortably like some of the stuff that the previous generation had struggled hard to get away from: sacramentalism, inadequate sermons, chants, pictures, ritual, incense, and so on. There is clearly a generational problem here! Many older church leaders struggle to work out why a new generation seems to be emerging with an agenda that seems so strikingly 'counter-revolutionary.' Where is this new agenda coming from?

From Modernism to Postmodernism

Alternative worship is far more postmodern in its cultural outlook than most forms of worship current in the church. Indeed, it is possible to describe the whole alternative worship scene as an attempt to inculturate Christian worship and church life. This needs to be looked at in some detail.

Postmodernism and postmodern culture are not exactly identical, but the points where they converge are some of the key defining features of the culture that is forming the new generation of adults in the West. These include:

1. Reducing the value placed on hard, logical, word-based reasoning.[22]
2. A tendency to move away from ultra-critical stances to the world in favour of more affirmative, open-ended, and open-minded approaches.[23]
3. An increasing suspicion of centralized structures of authority in favour of more local, *ad hoc*, and community-based structures.[24]
4. A continued openness to *individual experience* as a guide, but without trusting it implicitly or absolutely.[25]
5. A questioning of the whole post-enlightenment doctrine of 'progress.'

All of these features have exerted an influence on alternative worship, as they have on the cultural outlook of many young adults.

The first two features listed above have led to what has been described as the 're-enchantment' of the world. With the decline in the cultural significance of logic and reason, people are far more open now to spiritual, mystical, and magical components in everyday reality. This helps us to understand why the New Age has grown into such a large cultural force. It also helps us to understand the reappearance of a kind of sacramentality in alternative worship. If the modernist mindset tended to make a sharp distinction between the world of physics and the world of God, the postmodern mindset brings the world of the spirit back into the world of physical things. This also explains a key distinction between most charismatic worship and alternative worship. In charismatic worship, God is located 'outside' the physical domain, so to experience God means to experience him 'outside' or beyond the physical domain. This is why charismatic worship is so focussed on ecstatic experience. By contrast, alternative worship relocates God back within the physical domain, so to experience God means to encounter him in and through the created things around—symbolically, iconically, sacramentally.

This is not to say that alternative worship confuses God with the created order (although some, particularly those who follow Matthew Fox's writings, appear

---

22 Often referred to as the rejection of 'logocentrism.'
23 I Hassan ('The culture of postmodernism' in *Theory, Culture and Society*, 2 (3), pp 123–4) contrasts the modern/postmodern divide at this point with the contrasting terms, *paranoia* (the modern stance—not believing until proven) with *schizophrenia* (the postmodern stance—capable of holding mutually contradictory notions).
24 Drawn from the writings of M Foucault, who overturned the modern, enlightenment claim that co-operative centralization, based on reason and technology, would bring about human liberty. Foucault argued that rational thought could just as easily be pressed into the service of gaining power for a few.
25 This contrasts with the perspective of *existentialism* in late-modernity. The postmodern suspicion of the subjectivism of enlightenment philosophy cuts the ground out from under the feet of modern existentialism. Postmodern thought has nothing to put in the place of individual experience, but it constantly subverts it, doubts it, and ironizes it.

to flirt with pantheism). Rather, it is no longer being steered by modern culture into a rejection of the possibility of encountering God in and through one's createdness and physical environment. At a more popular level, this approach to spirituality reflects contemporary ecology in seeing creation in a much more positive light than much Christian theology has done in the past.

Theologically, this return to sacramentalism is accompanied by a renewed emphasis on the significance of the incarnation. The two are related, for in each God is seen as embracing the creation as his own. This relationship between sacramentalism and the incarnation can be traced back at least to Irenaeus in the 2nd century AD.[26] In the spirituality of alternative worship, young Christians are rediscovering and celebrating God's 'yes' to the earth in both creation and redemption. This affirmative sacramental stance also reflects something of the *schizophrenic* aspect of postmodernism,[27] which seems happy to embrace the intellectual and spiritual paradox of God taking human form in the comparative freedom of a postmodern cultural climate.

Experiential Ambivalence

Alternative worship is also postmodern by being much more ambivalent about the experiential side of worship, even though it remains central. Personal experience is welcomed, but not made into an absolute touchstone by which we can be sure we have met with God. There is more deliberate (some would say, honest) manipulation of worship experiences expressed through constructing rituals and symbolism. There is almost an ironic stance to the experiences of worship—often expressed in group jokes, and the tendency of alternative worship groups to lampoon themselves—which reflects the postmodern uncertainty about subjectivity. ('I know I'm having an enjoyable experience. I don't know for sure where it's coming from. I cannot say with certainty whether it is, or is not God.') The emerging generation of adults is sometimes known as the 'chemical generation.' Through the recreational use of drugs, many young people 'arrange' different personal experiences as a mode of self-expression. This is a much more mechanized approach to experience than the more 'spiritual' use made of LSD by their parents' generation. Alternative worship's ambivalent approach to experience therefore may be reflecting a wider cultural change in how personal experience is viewed philosophically and manipulated pharmacologically.

The word 'progress' was once almost coterminous with the word 'modern.' People would hanker after a nice modern house, and, in a similar way, whole churches would hanker after a nice modern liturgy. The result would be the same: progress—things would move on, and, it was presumed, get better. This myth lies shattered on the postmodern landscape. People still starve in Africa, nuclear weapons can destroy the world in a day, and post-war industry and transport

---

26 'And because we are his members and are nourished by what is created he...provides us with a created thing [the eucharist]' (Irenaeus, *Against the Heretics* V.2.2.3 arguing particularly against gnosticism and docetism).
27 See note on Hassan above.

have left us with the prospect of the world burning up or poisoning itself. The effects of this disenchantment are widespread, and it has left a mark on worship. Amongst alternative worshippers, there is a noticeable lack of interest in updating liturgies. Many groups use traditional language and symbolism with enthusiasm. 'Celtic' liturgies are preferred to the latest offerings of General Synod, partly because their language is more experiential and immediate, but also because liturgy produced by a centralized, modern bureaucracy is deemed unlikely to have anything authentic to offer. Indeed, the flatness of official liturgical language is seen as confirmation of the in-authenticity of liturgical bureaucracy.

This scepticism may also explain another key difference between alternative worship and charismatic spirituality. Implicit in much of the current charismatic scene is a sense that God is dealing with the church in step-by-step sequences: first-wave, second-wave, third-wave, Kansas City prophets, the Toronto Blessing, Pensacola, and so on. Each phase marks a step forward for the church.[28] To the postmodern mind, there seems to be more than a little of the modernist doctrine of progress in all this. Many Christians involved in alternative worship are weary of a spirituality that seems to be driven by a cultural obsession with the latest, newest, best.

But Is It all 'New Age?'

Some church leaders are concerned at what they see as 'New Age' elements present in alternative worship. There are points of resemblance—the use of ritual, the emphasis on ecology and creation, the use made of the imagination and tactile experience. These are not accidental: both alternative worship and New Age are responding to aspects of the postmodern culture they both inhabit. But New Age functions as the 'folk-religion' of postmodernity—it is unencumbered by any orthodoxy or tradition. It can therefore develop free, and foster a whole range of practices and claims, which people may take up, try, and even perhaps believe in.

By contrast, alternative worship is working from a particular understanding of the world that is shaped by the belief that God has acted uniquely in Jesus Christ. It remains part of the church, so has to negotiate between innovation and faithfulness to tradition, between the limits of the wider Christian community and the need to adapt to a new cultural context. This brings tensions that do not exist for the 'New Ager.' Christians of a radical mindset need to be aware that were it not for these tensions, however irksome, their religion could end up being just another piece of fractured belief floating in the ocean of the New Age.

Therefore, Christians who look at alternative worship from the outside should try to realize that some of the 'similarities' between alternative worship and 'New Age' are more cultural than doctrinal. At the same time, those within alternative worship need to realize (if they do not already) how difficult it is to tread the line between cultural appropriation and doctrinal assimilation.

---

28 'Step by step we're moving forward, little by little gaining ground...' (Doug Horley, *We want to see Jesus lifted high* ©1993 Thankyou Music.)

6
Responding to Alternative Worship

Although alternative worship is not a 'movement' on the scale of charismatic renewal, in those places where it has been fostered, it has attracted significant numbers from an age-group and cultural milieu which is normally significantly absent in many churches. Members of alternative worship congregations are integrated with some cultural enclaves that see very little Christian witness. So what lessons are being learnt, and how should the wider church respond?

Recognizing the Impact of a Cultural Sea-change

Western society is divided into many different sub-cultures, which in their turn are sub-divided into cultural enclaves. Also, young adults are more affected by the general move to cultural postmodernity than any other group. A generation is therefore growing up which feels disconnected from the culture of mainstream church. This culture-shift creates a widening gulf between young adults and those church structures, institutions and spiritualities which benefited from, and were shaped by the culture of late modernity. This includes the present liturgical structures of the Church of England, the charismatic renewal and resurgent evangelicalism.

This change brings new priorities, new battles and different needs—most especially in terms of spirituality. If the wider church is to take the pastoral and mission needs of a new generation seriously, then it should welcome the sort of innovation and creativity that alternative worship presently offers. It should accept that changes of practice, and of spiritual and theological emphasis are desirable and inevitable. It should not be threatened into an adversarial or reactive stance towards young people who have comparatively little power and influence within the church.

The increase in cultural diversity challenges churches to reflect a plural social context, whilst expressing an essential unity in Christ. We have grown used to an emphasis on Christian unity that insists on it being expressed through liturgical uniformity, preferably within a single congregation at a single service. This emphasis was particularly associated with the Liturgical Movement earlier this century. Yet it has also been experienced as an alienating, rather than a unifying force, not just by alternative worshippers, but by many others over the years.[29] One pressing challenge to the Church of England is how seriously it is going to ascribe integrity to the huge cultural range present in British society. In most local churches,

---

29 Supporters of threatened 8am communions and evensong found in them a cultural alternative to the often bland parish communion or family service, where many, especially the old or the childless, found themselves out on a limb spiritually and liturgically. Postmodern philosophy offers a compelling critique of this kind of collectivist ideology, accusing it of cultural totalitarianism by the empowered majority at the expense of the less powerful minority.

this question seems to be more urgent than the need to 'symbolize unity' through a common service of worship catering to the lowest common cultural denominator. Does such a thing exist anyway? Is it not rather the cultural group that traditionally has had most influence? In cities and large towns, there is a growing trend for churches or congregations to exist as single cultural units. Should this trend be accepted, or is it a form of cultural slavery to market forces?

Churches of an evangelical or charismatic ethos also face a further challenge: the shift to postmodernity may be rendering some aspects of their present spirituality irrelevant, dated, or offensive. This effect features regularly in the life stories of many of those who have become involved with alternative worship. It is why Roland Howard describes alternative worship as 'the bastard child of the charismatic renewal.'[30] Some alternative worship groups have faced most opposition from those same 'traditional' charismatic churches that nurtured them in their youth. Despite events such as *Soul Survivor*, the fall-out at full adulthood appears to remain high. Some of these 'casualties' are making their way into alternative worship groups, but there is also evidence that still more are becoming involved in New Age and neo-pagan groups. Both resurgent evangelicalism and the charismatic renewal benefited from the culture of late-modernity. Time will tell whether they have the foresight to invest in those developments and new agendas that engage fully with postmodernity.

The Challenge of Liturgical Creativity

If alternative worship were simply a matter of a new style of music, symbols or architecture it would pose no serious challenge to the established Anglican way of doing things in liturgy. The problem is that its approach to doing worship is much more holistic. An alternative worship group takes an interest and responsibility for the entire 'text' of its worship. This embraces those aspects that the Church of England currently manages centrally: the ritual structure and the text of prayers. There has been an explosion of creative writing and ritual construction within alternative worship alongside developments in graphics and symbolism. This creates a dilemma: should an Anglican group keep their hands off one part of the 'text' of their alternative worship—the written prayers of the liturgy?

Anglican theology since the 1970s has re-emphasized the importance of liturgy for Anglican identity. Unfortunately, this has led to a general attitude of conservation and the need to 'rein-in' too much local variation, driven by the fear that variation in liturgy will weaken church theological identity.[31] Yet this stress on liturgical conservatism in the interests of doctrinal stability has turned Anglican self-understanding on its head, because it leaves the Church of England's

---

30 Roland Howard, *Charismania* (London: Mowbray, 1997).
31 This 'reining-in' approach lay behind the desire to bring non-sacramental family services into canonical provision through the authorization of *A Service of the Word*. Although *A Service of the Word* gave more *official* leeway than ever before, one is left wondering whether *any* Sunday act of worship now falls beyond liturgical provision to be subject to a local priest's liturgical discretion, including alternative worship. The 'bureaucrats' may have got it all sewn-up!

traditional understanding of its mission out of the picture. The result is uncomfortably close to urging the Church to mutate into a conservative liturgical sect instead of evolving its worship in ways that allow it to remain a church that embraces the diversity of contemporary society, the lax as well as the fervent. This inclusive vision is very close to what many alternative worship groups are currently trying to do. The current climate in the Church of England, however, appears not as conducive to liturgical experimentation as it has been in the past.

Another problem with this approach is that the cultural context gives it very little support. It effectively places a chastity belt around the *words* of the rite, whilst allowing the hymnody, symbolism, and other aspects of the worship to act, at times, very promiscuously. But if the words of worship are no longer *experienced* as its defining feature, then where does that leave the unique focus of Anglican identity? Furthermore, it is quite possible, within a multi-media context, to subvert or even lampoon the sentiments of the spoken word. For example, *TSS* have used ironic visual subversion with a video loop of Charlie Chaplin being swallowed up by a machine in the film *Modern Times* played over words which talked about the wonderful feat of human technological achievement. More insidious subversion of the spoken words is possible. Imagine playing a clip from *Spitting Image* during the traditional state prayers for the government and royal family!

Obviously, the possibilities of alteration or subversion of the theology of liturgical texts expand in a multi-media environment. Yet it is arguable that this also happens in more traditional forms of worship. One example of this is in singing the lyrics of non-Anglican hymnody, such as some of the choruses from a Restoration house church stable which imply the extinction of traditional denominations. Another is the use made by 19th century Anglo-catholics of the ceremonial of the Roman Mass whilst using the words of the BCP. Both illustrate that the words of liturgy only form belief to a limited extent. The current desire to preserve Anglican identity through the centralized control of the words of liturgical prayer flounders in practice. The only practical way this could be achieved is if the hymnody, architecture and symbolism of the rite were all subject to a similar centralized control. Young people are growing up in a world of interacting symbols and signs, where heavy use is made of irony and subversion. They are becoming competent in the grammar of a multi-media communicative dialect. An Anglican insistence that writing the prayers of liturgy remains the prerogative of a centralized liturgical 'expertise' comes over as patronizing and artificial. The time may be ripe for an ironic onslaught.

For years, liturgists have struggled with a liturgical 'deflation' in which they tried to ensure that charismatic Anglicans used at least a modicum of ritual and liturgy. How should they now cope with a liturgical 'inflation' by alternative worshippers enthusiastically composing liturgies of their own, in which the words form an integral part of a multi-media rite that cannot be detached from it?

When alternative worship happens in the Church of England, most diocesan bishops welcome it, but normally adopt the stance of 'please don't tell me what you're doing'—since to do so would implicate the bishop in non-canonical liturgy. Yet this approach forces the activity of alternative worship groups underground and weakens their relationship with the wider church and the accountability of the group or its leaders. This policy is pastorally unwise, for it weakens church unity, confuses the group's identity, and impedes the effectiveness of the group's mission. Yet as things stand, canon law and the present structures of liturgical authorization are working together to keep alternative worship out of full relationship with the Church of England.

Rethinking the Structures

In the medium to long-term, the only realistic way through these problems would be to replace the current (modern) structures of centralized liturgical production with more local ones. These would place more emphasis on resourcing and guiding churches as they built worship together locally. This would not rule out using traditional texts, such as the BCP, but as resources rather than as complete rites. In such a context, the local clergy would act, under the bishop's jurisdiction, as advisers to creative groups. Their job would be to ensure that any innovation reflected the Anglican tradition enshrined in the traditional liturgical texts. In this way, advice could be given within a pastoral relationship built on friendship, trust and encouragement. At the same time, central bodies, such as the Liturgical Commission, could be charged with producing new resources which demonstrated an Anglican 'norm,' serving as models rather than as prescriptions. The job of the Liturgical Commission would be to disseminate contextual examples of good practice rather than to compose out of context.

The growing dissatisfaction with the current round of liturgical revision felt by many churches suggests that we are dealing with a system suffering cultural obsolescence. A serious rethink is now needed. Alternative worship is reflecting, in one particularly acute way, a wider cultural turn against a sense of 'cultural presumptuousness' in the methods of a centralized bureaucracy. This change is being felt, not just by younger people, but across the age-range. Liturgy has always been central to the spirituality of Anglicanism. But in our present cultural climate, for that spirituality to become again the spirituality of the people of our church, our liturgy must become again a 'work of the people.' The example of alternative worship offers a way forward for the rest of the church.